PAṬṬINAPPĀLAI

KAṬIYALUR
URUTHIRAṄ KAṆṆAṆĀR

MJP
PUBLISHERS

PAṬṬINAPPĀLAI

KAṬIYALŪR
URUTHIRAṄ KAṆṆANĀR

Translated by

R. VENKATARAMAN, Ph.D

Formerly Professor of English, Annamalai University,
Professor and Head, Department of English,
SCSVMV, Kanchipuram and Professor and Head,
Department of English VELS University
Pallavaram, Chennari – 600 117.

Chennai   New Delhi

ISBN 9789355279774   MJP Publishers

All rights reserved   No. 44, Nallathambi Street,

Printed and bound in India   Triplicane, Chennai 600 005

MJP 1658   Publishers, 2024

Publisher : C. Janarthanan

Project Editor : C. Ambica

PREFACE

My habit in getting to sleep at night is to read some book for fifteen minutes to half-an-hour. It was on one such occasion I chanced to read *Pattinappālai,* an edition of which a friend asked me to keep safe promising to have it from me later. Instead of sleep, there arose an awakening in me due to the swift metrical run of the poem which sent down in me a throb. Though I did not understand the content of the lines, I started realizing the poeticity in them, both deliberate and natural. Hence, I started collecting dictionaries, and annotated editions of the song, and determined to lend a patient study. This eventually infused in me certain phraseologies which I felt proud to use while taking to my friends in the Tamil department of my institution Annamalai University. They started looking at me with doubt about my wits and latterly understood the spell of influence I was in. There arose a thought in me in the meanwhile about translating the work. Some discouraged me, and some half-heartedly encouraged me. However, I was determined in my task. I was sure that I would not be able to do justice to the rhythm of the song it throbs with in Tamil. However, I took to translate it making use of free verse, the safe repository when one finds difficulties in imparting the original cadence in the translated language. The purpose of any translation has two primary aims: i) to give an expose to the asapects of the original work, This is to transfer the inhernet culture present in the original work and also to the literary techniques that exhibit the nuances of the language in the original text. However, the expose to the latter aspects depends on the intellectual prowess of the translator. Readers interested in the linguistic and prosodic aspects in translation constitute only a very lean percentage. Translation of texts has been going on right from the ancient times and theories of translation and their application are to be found only in the modern times. As regards translation of poetry, Stephen Spender's advice sounds relevant: "... a poet's aim as a translator should not be absolutely necessary, but to return to the source of the poet's inspiration and to create a parallel poem in the English Language".

I must admit that I was driven more by impulse than by any translation theory though what I have done may fit into some theory characterizing the poetic lines. I feel that the readers will not be disappointed at what I have attempted.

My thanks are due to Dr.E. Manamaran, a Senior faculty of the Department of History, Annamalai University without whose goading I would not have attempted this publication. I thank the MJP Publishers, Chennai - 600 005 for their interest in this work and meticulousness in execution.

Next, I thank Dr.L.Thirunavukkarasu, Hon.Professor of English, Alagappa University, Karaikkudi for his consistent encouragement to my endeavour.

– R. Venkataraman

Scheme of Translation

அ	a	ஞ்	ñ
ஆ	ā	ட்	ṭ
இ	ī	ண்	ṇ
ஈ	ī	த்	t
உ	u	ந்	n
ஊ	ū	ப்	p
எ	e	ம்	m
ஏ	ē	ய்	y
ஐ	ai	ர்	r
ஒ	o	ல்	l
ஓ	ō	வ்	v
ஔ	au	ழ்	ḻ
ஃ	x	ள்	ḷ
க்	k	ற்	ṟ
ங்	ṅ	ன்	ṉ
ச்	c		

CONTENTS

INTRODUCTION

Literature of the *Caṅkam* period in the ancient Tamil land is what is called *Caṅkam* literature which in epithetical expression is classical literature. It is believed that there existed three *Caṅkams* in the ancient Tamil land which congregated periodically, analysed and researched in depth the Tamil language. The poets of those ages were wont to sing on the internal (*akam*) and external subjects (*puram*), the former pertaining to the imaginative aspects of love, and the latter recognizing and extolling heroism, eleemosynary tendencies, fame and such aspects of life. In conformity with this tradition, in songs of the internal known as *akappaṭalkaḷ* there is celebration of love between the imaginative lovers – the male referred to as *talaivaṉ*, and the female as *talaivi*. Songs of the external – the *puṟappaṭalkal* extol the heroism of the king, his charity and munificence, the rare deeds of citizens and so on. While songs of the internal are imaginative, those of the external tell of facts and hence contribute to history too.

In the absence of transportation and hence lack of interaction among people living in towns and villages in the ancient Tamil land, people had to be contented living where they were (in mountains, hills, forests, farm lands sea shores) earning their livelihood by means of hunting, farming, fishing etc. The regions where they lived were known as *Kuṟiñci* (mountains and hills), *Mullai* (forest), *Marutam* (farm land), *Neital* (seashore), and *Pālai* (mountain and forest benefit of wealth). To people in these regions, love and the eventual codified life were of supreme concern in a natural way. Folk literature of the respective regions had for its central theme the love-life of the people concerned. In such a context, depending upon regions, the objects of first concern in literature was nature, and occupation of people. The property of literature was love as it was considered the prime of life bereft of which nature and occupation were deemed futile. Those objects demonstrative of such a life were treated as the nucleus of existence. As customs and habits, culture and attitudes differed from region to region, the songs also differed in their subject matter. No song of the *Caṅkam* period celebrates nature exclusively. Every song was sung indispensably with the enfoldment of love juxtaposed with rich descriptions of nature. Tradition had it that love was blended with imagination and against its absence the benevolence and heroism of kings were sung.

Songs of the internal and those of the external were classified and sung according to the regions and activities namely *Vetci, Vāñci, Uḻiñai, Tumpai, Vākai Pāṭān, Kāñci, Kaikkiḷai* and *Peruntinai. Vetci* marks the activity of possessing the cows of the enemy king thereby setting the prelude for war. Invading the enemy's land is *Vanci.* Beseiging the fort of the enemy is *Ulinai. Tumpai* pertains to waging war in dispute to a specific place. Victory refers to *Vākai. Pāṭān* speaks of victory in glorifying terms. The transitory nature of the world is conveyed by *Kāñci. Kaikkiḷai* reveals one sided love and *Peruntiṇai* tells of unequal love between lovers. The songs of *Caṅkam* literature revolve around these aspects concerning both the internal (*akam*) and external (*puṟam*).

Eṭṭuttokai

Collectively called *Eṭṭuttokai*, this enfolds five works containing songs pertaining to thoughts internal. These are *Akanāṉūṟu, Naṟṟiṇai, Kuṟuntokai, Aiṅkuṟunūṟu, and Kalittokai*. All these sing of imaginative love. *Paripāṭal* is highly musical in nature, and deals with love and worship of God. *Patiṟṟuppattu* praises ten *Cēra* Kings. *Puṟanāṉūṟu* contains songs that glorify the worthy deeds and rare traits of the ancestors of the Tamil land.

Nature Poetry

English literature abounds in exclusive poetry that takes cognizance of the spiritual, physical and mental impact that nature is capable of exerting on the human psyche. The Romantic poets of the late 18th and early 19th centuries spiritualised, supernaturalised, sensualised, and intellectualized Nature as could be experienced in the poetry of Wordsworth, Coleridge, Keats and Shelley respectively. Walter Scott blended history with nature and presented altogether a different dimension in his poetry and novels too. Such a kind of exclusive treatment of nature is not to be found in *Caṅkam* poetry even though it is an aspect endowed with rich and succulent descriptions. However, *Nature* was subordinated to love, heroism and benevolence. But what was sung provide us with rare sights and experiences and appeal to our aesthetic sensibility. The ancient Tamil poets were given names depending upon the nature of such descriptions.

Background Descriptions as Tradition

In *Caṅkam* poetry, the descriptions of Nature serve as background to the main issues and this custom became established in later poetry. It is affirmed by critics that such background descriptions of nature could be seen in *Ātruppaṭai* poetry. The term *Ātruppaṭai* means leading the way or showing the way, a kind of instruction as to the modality of a particular kind of aspect of life. Natural descriptions blend with didacticism and facilitate easier reach to the mind of readers. The ten long songs, idyllic in nature in **Pattuppāṭṭu** including the *Ātruppaṭai* songs are of such a type. The **Pattuppāṭṭu** songs or idylls as they could be called, with nature as the backdrop, animate, demonstrate, and dramatize the emotion of the poets concerned and establish lyrical intensity.

Telling effect is created by these idylls with their pictorial and meticulous descriptive power aiding the vivifying visual exercise of the reader. Though the hierarchic order of their composition is uncertain, a song in Tamil enfolding them is of little guidance to us to order ourselves in analyzing them. This song in transliteration.

Muruku porunāṟu Paṇirantu Mullai

Peruku Vaḷamaturaik kāñci – maruviniya

Kōlaneṭu nalvāṭai kōluṟiñcip

Pālaikaṭattōṭum pattu

This song enables us to retain in our memory the ten songs or idylls. They are:

(1) Tirumurukāt̲r̲uppaṭai,   (2) Porunār̲āt̲r̲uppaṭai,

(3) Perumpāṇāt̲r̲uppaṭai,   (4) Cir̲upāṇāt̲ruppaṭai,

(5) Mullaippāṭṭu,   (6) Maturaikkāñci,

(7) Neṭunalvāṭai,   (8) Kur̲iñcippāṭṭu,

(9) Paṭṭinappālai,   (10) Malaipaṭukaṭām.

Tirumurukāt̲r̲uppaṭai (Guidance to worship Lord Murugan)

Nakkīrar sang this poem of 317 lines. It is in the form of guidance to those that wish to have the grace of Lord *Murukan̲*. Brimming with spiritual devotion, this happens to be the full fledged divinely devotional song of the *Cân̲kam* times. Teeming with descriptions of nature, it details out Lord (God) *Murukan̲'s* appearance, his abodes, the war he waged with *Cûran̲*, the characteristics of saints and women who offered him worship and the customs of the people of hilly regions in their nature of worship unto the Lord.

Porunār̲āt̲r̲uppaṭai (Guidance to a Bard)

This poem is of 248 lines written by *Muṭattama Kaṇṇiyar*, and celebrates the affection that *Karikāla n̲* showed unto musicians called *Porunar*. Their music played on the ya l̲ was of such mellifluity that even murderers who were out to burgle them were transformed of their diabolic designs. *Karikāla n̲* used to provide such musicians with rich clothes, gossamer like silks, gold etc.

Ciṟupāṇātruppaṭai (Guidance to a Bard)

There is meticulous depiction of poverty and impoverishment of all sorts that suffered a class of musicians called *Pāṇar*. Running 269 lines, this poem by *Nattattanar* tells of the sense of prestige and dignity of such musicians who though impecunious in state, never descended down to the level of entreaty unto anyone for money. Their want was to approach only those that were benevolent and philanthropic, that too after being assured of such traits in them by their fellow musicians.

Perumpāṇātruppaṭai (Guidance to a Bard)

This song by *Uruttiraikaṇṇanār* of 500 lines pays tribute to one *Iḷantiraiyan* who was ruling *Kāñci*. The poem speaks of the state, the sea-shore town, the light house, and the king's traits as an unflinching host.

Mullaippāṭṭu (Woodland Song)

Love and nature find splendorous manifestation in this poem of 103 lines by *Nappūtanar*. As the title indicates, in conformity with the possessive characteristic of the region, the lady-love is pining for her male lover who has departed to fulfil his duty as a soldier. The time of return is the probable rainy season. When it is on, the lady love comes concerned, and she hears the sound of her man's chariot approaching. There is luscious description of beauty that the forest lands acquire during the rainy season.

Maturaikkāñci (A Song on Mathurai)

Mānkuṭi Marutanār sang this poem of 782 lines, the longest in *Pattuppāṭṭu*. It is didactic in the sense that it tells of the transitory nature of life and emphasizes the righteous path in life. Since this was addressed to *Pāntiyan Neṭuñceliyan* who was ruling from *Maturai,* it was named *Maturaik Kāñci.* The city of Maturai is described in diverse ways in the poem.

Neṭunalvāṭai (A Long Gold Wind)

This is yet *Nakkīrar's* another long poem of 188 lines that celebrates imaginative love in the form of the pining female lover worshipping the Goddess *Koṭravai (Kāli)* to bestow victory on her male lover who has gone to war, so that he could return early to dispel her distress. In fact this is a prayer song juxtaposed with the description of the wafting cold wind.

Kuṟiñcippāṭṭu (Mountain Idyll)

This poem was composed by poet *Kapilar* to instruct a northern king *Prakattan* about the tradition of Tamil literature. It has 261 lines that speak of true love which never runs smooth. As indicated by the title, there run descriptions of the mountain land (*Kuṟiñci*).

Paṭṭinappālai (Song on City and Seperation)

Kaṭiyalūr Uruttirankaṇṇanar composed this song of 301 lines. It speaks of the male lover's intended separation on account of earning wealth, and his lady-love lamnenting over his separation. The poet's poeticity is to be experienced in the descriptions of *Kāviri Pūmpaṭṭinam* and the fame of *Karikāl Cōlaṉ*. The male lover on the verge of his departure realizes that even if he were to be blessed with the rich and flourishing *Pūmpaṭṭinam,* he would not leave his lady-love whose shoulders are far more blissful than the sceptre of the king *Karikālaṉ. Kāviripūmpaṭṭinam is* also known as *Pukār* and this is known as *Pūmpaṭṭinam.* Leaving this area meant passage into mountain and forest land bereft of wealth signifying *Pālai.* Hence the title *Paṭṭinappālai.* It is also called *Vancineṭumpaṭṭu.*

Malaipaṭukaṭām (Echo of a Mountain)

Perumkaucikanâr wrote this poem of 583 lines. This is also called *Kūtaratṟuppaṭai.* The mountain becomes a metaphor for the elephant here and the description pertains to various sounds that emanate from the mountain. These sounds are deemed reflective of the musth of the elephant. The main theme, however, is the artful life of a seat of musicians known as *Kūttar.*

Theme of – Paṭṭinappālai

In order to demonstrate the innermost intensity of affection of the male lover for his lady-love, the poet intelligently makes use of external descriptions to extol the glory of *Pūmpukār* and then makes the male lover declare that he would at no cost be lost to his lady. Such a declaration constitutes only a scanty part of the poem despite that being the crux. Hence the *akam* or the internal, though purposive, loses its significance at the cost of *puram* or the external that is picturesquely lyrical accounting for the idyllic nature of the poem.

Social History

The picture of the river *Kāviri,* the life of people around, their customs, habits, religious attitude, the monarch's state, administration and wealth find goodly treatment and they vouch for the splendour of the ancient Cōḷa Kingdom. The reader is spellbound by the rhythm of cadence contributed by *Kalippā* and *Vañcippā,* the former containing eight feet of two syllables each, and the latter of six feet of two syllables each. Analysing the prosody of the poem one finds that *Vañcippā* dominates the poetic lines and hence another title for it–*Vañcippāṭṭu.* As regards the date of composition, *Pattuppāṭṭu* in general, and *Paṭṭiṉappālai* in particular, there is no availability of credible material. Anyhow, Tamil scholars of eminence believe that these ten songs (idylls) must have been composed between the first, and third century A.D.

காவிரியின் சிறப்பு

வசையில்புகழ் வயங்கு வெண்மீன்
திசைதிரிந்து தெற்கேகினும்
தன்பாடிய தளிஉணவின்
புள்தேம்பப் புயல்மாறி
5   வான்பொய்ப்பினும் தான்பொய்யா
மலைத்தலைய கடல்காவிரி

சோழ நாட்டு மருத வளம்

புனல்பரந்து பொன்கொழிக்கும்
விளைவறா வியன்கழனிக்
கார்க்கரும்பின் கமழாலைத்
10   தீத்தெறுவின் கவின்வாடி
நீர்ச்செறுவின் நீள்நெய்தல்
பூச்சரம்பும் புலத்தாங்கண்
காய்ச்செந்நெல் கதிர் அருந்தும்
மோட்டெருமை முழுக்குழவி
15   கூட்டுநிழல் துயில்வதியும்

Kaviriyin Cirappu

Vasaiil pukaḻ vayaṅku veṇmīṉ
Thisaithirintu therkēkiṉum
Tanpāṭiya thaḷi uṇaviṉ
Puḷthēmpap puyalmāṟi
Vāṉpoyppiṉum tāṉpoyyā
Malaitalaiya kaṭal kāviri

Cōlaṉāttu Marutavaḷam

Puṉalparantu poṉkoḷikkum
Viḷaivarā viyaṉkaḷanik
Kārkkarumpiṉ kamaḷālait
Titteruvin kaviṉvāṭi
Nīrceruviṉ nīḷ neital
Pūccāmpum pulattaṉkaṉ
Kāycennal katir aruntum
Moṭṭerumai muḻukkuḷavi
Kūṭṭuniḻal tuyilvatiyum

Magnificence of the Kāviri (1-7)

Even if Venus sparkling with blemishless stance
Unto southward drift off its custom's course,
And though rains, skylark-cheered, fail in shower
Much to the bird's woe negating its feed
The *Kāviri* which begins from mountain top   (5)
Belies not, flowing ocean-like, amassing
Golden wealth on spread of sands.

Agricultural Wealth of the Cōla State (8-20)

The lands are wide and far, never bereft of yield;
Juice of verdant luscious canes of sugar
Waft with fragrance from boiling pans,   (10)
And there the heat of smoke withers bad
The *Neital* flowers long; in shadows of paddy heaps
Lie in slumber, calves of bellied buffaloes
Feed on paddy grains dry, red and ripe.
Here in plenteous state stand with fruits   (15)
In clusters and huddles coconut trees
And banana plants together with areca palms
Of bunchy yield along with fragrant turmeric
And mangoes rich of pedigree, and clumpy palms
Rooty rhizome and shoots of ginger.   (20)

கோள்தெங்கின் குலைவாழைக்
காய்க்கமுகின் கமழ்மஞ்சள்
இனமாவின் இனர்ப்பெண்ணை
முதல்செம்பின் முளை இஞ்சி
20   அகன்நகர் வியன்முற்றத்துச்
சுடர்நுதல் மடநோக்கின்
நேரிழை மகளிர் உணங்குணாக் கவரும்
கோழி எறிந்த டிகாடுங்கால் கனங்கழை
பொன்கால் புதல்வர் புரவியின் றுருட்டும்
25   முக்கால் சிறுதேர் முன்வழி விலக்கும்
விலங்குபகை அல்லது கலங்குபகை அறியாக்
கொழும்பல்குடிச் செழும்பாக்கத்துக்
குறும்பல்லூர் நெடுஞ்சோணாட்டு

பட்டினத்தின் பெருமைகள்
தோட்டம் பொழில் பொய்கை

வெள்ளை உப்பின் கொள்ளை சாற்றி
30   நெல்லொடு வந்த வல்வாய்ப் பஃறி

Panṭṭiṇattin Perumaikaḷ
Tōṭṭam, Poḻil, Poykai

Veḷḷai uppiṉ koḷḷai sāṭri
Nelloṭ vanta valvāyp paṭri

Kōḷteṅkiṉ kulaivāḷaik
Kāykkamukiṉ kamaḷmañcaḷ
Iṉamāviṉ iṉarppeṇṇai
Muthalsempiṉ muḷai iñci
Akaṉṉakar viyanmuṭrattuc
Cuṭarnutal maṭaṉōkkiṉ
Nēriḷai makaḷir uṇaṅkuṇāk kavarum
Kōḷi erinta kotuṅkāl kaṇaṅkuḷai
Poṉkāl putalvar puraviyiṉ ṛuruttum
Mukkāl ciruter munvaḷi vilakkum
Vilaṅkupakai allathu kalaṅkupakai ariyāk
Koḷumbalkutic ceḷumpākkattuk
Kurumpallūr ṉetunchoṇattu

Wealth of the Cōlā Farmland (21-28)

In courtyards of stretched out expanse
Of houses, demoiselles of radiant foreheads
and Looks naive, with befitting jewelry
Hurl earrings in solid gold and in twirls
At hens and cocks that feed on drying paddy.   (25)
Block these jewels in turn the horseless chariots small
On three wheels by urchins rolled, wearing anklets
                                           gold;
Save this hostile stance no rattling feud blots
The life of diverse tribes in the coastal Cōla state
Rich with hamlets abutting each other dear.   (30)

Pukār's Groves, Gardens and Lakes (29-39)

This land has ambient groves where boats sturdy
On turn with paddy bartered for whitely salt
Are fastened firm to trunks of trees that
Liken stallions haltered at stables secure.

பணைநிலைப் புரவியின் அணைமுதல் பிணிக்கும்
கழிசூழ் படப்பைக் கலியாணர்ப்
பொழில்புறவின் பூந்தண்டலை
மழைநீங்கிய மாவிசும்பின்
35   மதிசேர்ந்த மகவெண்மீன்
உருகெழுதிறல் உயர்கொட்டத்து
முருகமர்பூ முரண்கிடக்கை
வரியணிசுடர் வான்பொய்கை
இருகாமத்து இணையேரிப்

அட்டில் சாலைகள்

40   புலிப்பொறிப் போர்க்கதவில்
திருத்துஞ்சும் திண்காப்பின்
பிகழ்நிலைஇய மொழிவளர
அறம்நிலைஇய அகன் அட்டில்
சோறுவாக்கிய கொழுங்கஞ்சி
45   யாறுபோலப் பரந்தொழுகி
ஏறுபொரச் சேறாகித்

Panainilaip puravivin anaimutal pinikkum
Kalisulp patappaik kaliyanarp
Polilpuravin pūntantalai
Malainī nkiya māvisumpin
Mathisērnta makavenmīn
Urukeluthiral uyarkōttattu
Murukamarpū murankitakkai
Varianisutar vānpoykai
Irukāmathu inaiērip

Attil Sālaikal

Pulipporip pōrkkatavil
Tiruttuncum tinkāppin
Pikalnilaiiya molivalara
Aramnilaiiya akan attil
Sōruvākkiya kolunkañci
Yarupōlap paranttoluki
Eruporac cērakit

Furtherance are gardens flowery, bordering groves   (35)
That earn income new that stems swagger straight.
There's a tank with sturdy and soaring banks
Sembling the Moon when it company keeps
With *Makam,* a star luminous in *firmament* vast
Free of rainy clouds where *fragrant* blooms of   (40)
Diverse hues in contrast lie and painting make
Of the tank; there lakes are two that bless one
With boon of sensual pleasures, worldly this and other.

Kitchen Streets (40-50)

The town has valiant walls with Tiger mark
On gates in splendid amalgam blazoned;   (45)
Here grandeur reigns; there abound kitchens
That tributes shower and virtues affirm for
Yonder birth; brims out from these kitchens
Rich paste from boiling rice distilled that
Spreads, and flows rivulet-like and as bullocks   (50)
Vie to drink this, clash do they, and into
Slush it turns with soil blend that dries up
Rising dust as chariots racy run and

Like the elephant grimy in slush smeared, glimmers
The palace white with diverse paintings great.   (55)

தேரோடத் துகள்கெழுமி
நீறாடிய களிறுபொல
வேறுபட்ட வினைஒவத்து
50   வெண்கோயில் மாசூட்டும்

பல்வேறு இடங்கள்

தண்கேணித் தகைமுற்றத்துப்
பகட்டெருத்தின் பல்சாலைத்
தவப்பள்ளித் தாழ்காவின்
அவிர்சடை முனிவர் அங்கி வேட்கும்
55   ஆவுதி நறும்புகை முனைஇக் குயில்தம்
மாயிரும் பெடையோடு இரியல் போகிப்
பூதம் காக்கும் புகலரும் மடிநகர்த்
தூதணம் புறவொடு துச்சில் சேக்கும்

முரண்களரி

முதுமரத்த முரண்களரி
60   வரிமணல் அகன்திட்டை

Terōṭat tukaḷkeḻuumi
Nīraṭiya kaḷirupōla
Vērupaṭṭa viṉaiōvattu
Veṇkōil māsuṭṭum

Palvēṟu Iṭaṅkaḷ

Thaṇkēṉith thakaimutṟattup
Pakaṭṭeruttiṉ palsālait
Thavappaḷḷit tāḻkāvin
Avirsatai muṉivar anki vētkum
Āvuthi narumpukai muṉaiik kuyiltam
Māyirum petaiyōtu iriyal pōkip
Pūtham kākkum pukalarum matiṉakart
Tūthaṉam puravotu tuccil cēkkum

Muraṇkaḷari

Mutumaratta muraṇkaḷari
Varimaṉal akaṉthiṭṭai

Different Places of Pukār (51-58)

The town holds in its range within
Ponds chill of smaller forms and manifold yards
To hay-feed bullocks, and cloisters that repose
Give unto penancing hermits where with
Matty locks do they kindle sacred fire   (60)
And in oblation pour ghee and sundry
That lend scented smoke loathing which
Cuckoos in pairs with females black and proud
Flee in jitters and rest with pigeons that
Feed on smaller stones with repose in remoter parts   (65)
Where groves abound with verdant trees that
Lowly lie amidst where demons guard that makes

passage hard.

The War – Game Yard (59-74)

Amidst ancient trees lies the battle ground
On sandy highland with wind-made stripes
Where kinsmen warriors in war-game indulge   (70)

இருங்கிளை இனன்ஒக்கல்
கருந்தொழில் கலிமாக்கள்
கடல்இறவின் சூடுதின்றும்
வயல்ஆமைப் புழுக்குண்டும்
65 வறள்அடும்பின் மலர்மலைந்தும்
புனல் ஆம்பல் பூச்சூடியும்
நீள்நிறவிசும்பின் வலனேர்புதிரிதரு
நாள்மீன் விராயகோள்மீன் போல
மலர்தலைமன்றத்துப் பலருடன் குழீஇக்
70 கையினும் கலத்தினும் மெய்யுறத்தீண்டிப்
பெருஞ்சினத்தால் புறக்கொடாஅ(து)
இருஞ்செருவின் இகல்மொய்ம்பினோர்
கல்லெறியும் கவண்வெரீஇப்
புள்இரியும் புகர்ப்போந்தை

புறஞ்சேரியும் முன்றிலும்

75 புறழ்ப்பன்றிப் பல்கோரீ
ஊறைக்கிணற்றுப் புறச்சேரி

Irunkilai inaṉokkal
Karuntoḻil kalimākkaḷ
Kataliraviṉ cūtutiṉrum
Vayal āmaip puḻukkuṇṭum
Varaḷatumpiṉ malarmalaintum
Punal āmpal pūccūtiyum
Nīḷniravisumpiṉ valaṉērputiritaru
Naḷmīn virāyakōḷmīṉ pōla
Malartalaimaṉrattup palarutan kuliik
Kaiyinum kalatinum meyyurattiṉ tip
Peruñiṉattālpurakkotāa(tu)
Iruṅ ceruviṉ ikalmoympiṉor
KalleriyumKavaṇverīip
Puḷiriyum pukarppontai

Puṟañcĕrium Muṉṯrilum

Paraḷppanrip palkōri
Ūraikiṇatrup puraccĕri

By pride of valiance and bravery prompted,
Eating roasted shrimp, and turtle braised,
Sporting *Atumpu* blooms that on parched ground
Creep and *Āmpal* that on river side flourishment find;
Like stars and planets in welkin azure   (75)
Abreast go, the fighters and lookers
Throng on wider ground to gallantry gaze.
Warriors then in fight involve butting 'gainst each
In physical wrestle and duels armed
And turn irate when the foe recedes not.   (80)
Those with varied might, their strength manifest
In diverse tricks, shoot stones form slings
That birds frighten and blots dented make
On tufted palms that stand firm and strong.

The Outskirt Slum and Courtyard (75-83)

The slum that lies at *Pukār's* vicinage   (85)
Has pigs with shoats and assorted hens,
And curbed wells; there with partridges bucks do play.
There amidst firmed spears and ordered shields
Which like the fence to memorial stone appear,

Where amidst low-roofed huts fishing-drails   (90)
Are leaned; semblance bearing unto blemished moon
Fishing nets dry on sandy grounds expansive spread.

ஏழகத் தகரொடுவில்விளை யாடக்
கிடுகுநிரைத்து எஃகுஊன்றி
நடுகல்லின் அரண்போல
80   நெடுந்தூண்டிலில் காழ்சேர்த்திய
குறுங்கூரைக் குடிநாப்பண்
நிலவடைந்த இருள்போல
வலைஉணங்கும் மணல்முன்றில்

பரதவர் விழாவும் பொழுதுபோக்கும்

வீழ்த்தாழைத் தாள்காழ்ந்த
85   வெண்கூதாளத்துத் தண்பூங் கோதையர்
சினைச்சுறவின் கோடுநட்டு
மனைச்சேர்த்திய வல்லணங்கினான்
மடல்தாழைமலர்மலைந்தும்
பிணர்ப்பெண்ணைப் பிழிமாந்தியும்
90   புன்தலை இரும்பரதவர்
பைந்தழைமாமகளிரொடு
பாயிரும் பனிக்கடல் வேட்டம் செல்லாது

Eḻakat takarotuvilviḷaiyātak
Kitukuniraittu exkuūnri
Naṭukallin araṉ pōla
Netuntūntilil kāḻcertiya
Kurunkūraik kutināppaṉ
Nilavatainta iruḷpōla
Valaiuṇankum maṇalmunril

Paratavar Viḻāvum PoḻutuPōkkum

Vīḻtaḻait tāḷtāḻnta
Veṇkūtaḷattut taṉpūn kōtaiyar
Cinaiccuravin kōṭunattu
Manaiccertiya vallaṇankiṉān
Piṇarpeṇṇaip piḻimāntiyum
Puntalai irumparatavar
Paintāḻai māmakaḷiroṭu
Pāyirum panikkaṭal vēṭṭam cellatu

Fisher Festival and Pastime (84-105)

Fishermen rubious haired and sable skinned
Venture not on full moon day into the sea
High, and wide, black and cold; shun pangs emotive
(95)
And wear garlands of blooms of *Venṭāli*
Cool that under pines abound with hanging roots;
The folk firm on ground the horn of pregnant shark
Which with *screw-pine* flowers do they deck,
And on it the presence of *Varuṇan,* the Sea-God (100)
They do invoke, then sporting those blooms on self
They drink the sap of jagged palms unto Him offered.
They eat to their likes and play,
Tuned and towed by their crazy-go.
Then in the sandy shores that smell of meat   (105)
And florid spread where the sea of water clear
In tidal waves mall with the river *Kāviri*
Which likens unto amountain big on which
Clouds dark blanket wrap, and pectoral cling
The child makes unto its mother's breasts.   (110)
The fish folk do bath in sea to wash off sins
And in the river *Kāviri* take a dip
To rinse their salty skin. Shaking crabs
Do they play, and dance amidst spreading waves,
Making dolls of sand and 'joying senses sweet   (115)
To besotted state, and play with gusto all day long.

உவவுமடிந்து உண்டாடியும்
புலவுமணல் பூங்கானல்
95   மாமலைஅணைந்தகொண்மூப் போலவும்
தாய்முலை தழுவிய குழவி போலவும்
தேறுநீர்ப் புணரியோடு யாறுதலை மணக்கம்
மலிஒதத்து ஒலிகூடல்
தீதுநீங்கக் கடலாடியும்
100   மாசுபோகப் புனல்படிந்தும்
அலவன் ஆட்டியும் உரவுத்திரை உழக்கியும்
பாவை சூழ்ந்தும் பல்பொறிமருண்டும்
அகலாக் காதலொடு பகல்விளையாடிப்
105   பெறற்கருந் தொல்சீர்த் துறக்கம் ஏய்க்கும்
பொய்யாமரபின் பூமலி பெருந்துறை

கடைக்கங்குல்

துணைப்புணர்ந்த மடமங்கையர்
பட்டுநீக்கித் துகில்உடுத்து

Uvavumaṭintu uṇṭāṭiyum
Pulavu maṇal pūṅkānal
Māmalai anaintakoṇmūp pōlavum
Tāimulai taḻuviya kuḻavi pōlavum
Tēruṉīrp puṇariyōṭu yārutalai maṇakkum
Maliōtatu olikūṭal
Teetuṉiṅkak kaṭalaṭiyum
Māsupōkap punalpaṭintum
Alvaṉ āṭṭiyum uravuttirai uḻakkiyum
Pāvai cūḻntum palporimaruṇṭum
Akalāk kātaloṭu pakalviḷaiyaṭip
Perarkarun tolsīrt turakkam ēykkum
Poyyamarapin pūmali perunturai

Kataikkaṅkul

Tunaippuṇarnta maṭamaṅkaiyar
Paṭṭuṉīkkit tukiluṭuttu

A town it is that has bounteous blooms,
Holds tradition strong to unfailing luxuriance afford,
And pleasures rare and divine to provide,
Kāviri's firth does hold it vast and wide.   (120)

Last Lap of Night (106-115)

When departs dusk making way for dark,
From storeys high with pillars, tall men and maidens
Hear songs sweet of strain, watch plays with gusto
And delight derive that moonlight offers.
After this, guileless damsels with their males   (125)
Dalliance hold, and lingering still in that drowsy state

Cast of raiments silk to custom's robe;
Evade taking wine and revel in philtre drinks;
The garlands of males these damsels sport,
And that of damsels do their men wear;   (130)
In the last lap of night they all
Lapse into slumber deep and straight.
Fisherman who went into sea gaze
At storeys for lamps that flame still bright
And count them to time their turn unto the shore.(135)

மட்டுநீக்கி மதுமகிழ்ந்து
மைந்தர் கண்ணி மகளிர் சூடவும்
110 மகளிர் கோதை மைந்தர் மலையவும்
நெடுங்கால் மாடத்து ஒள்ளரி நோக்கிக்
கொடுந்திமில் பரதவர் குருஉச்சுடர் எண்ணவும்
பாடல் ஓர்ந்தும் நாடகம் நயந்தும்
வெண்ணிலவின் பயன்துய்த்தும்
115 கண்ணடைஇய கடைக்கங்குலான்

துறைமுகம்

மாஅகாவிரி மணம்கூட்டும்
தூஉஎக்கர்த் துயில்மடிந்து
வால்இணர் மடல்தாழை
வேல்ஆழி வியன்தெருவில்
120 நல்லிறைவன் பொருள்காக்கும்
தொல்லிசைத் தொழில்மாக்கள்
காய்சினத்த கதிர்ச்செல்வன்
தேர்பூண்ட மாஅபோல

Maṭṭunīkki matumakiḻntu
Maintar kaṇṇi makalir cūṭavum
Makalir kōtai maintar malaiyavum
Neṭuṅkāl māṭatu oḷari nōkkik
Koṭuntimil paratavar kurūucuṭar eṇṇavum
Pāṭ al ōrntum nāṭakam nayantum
Veṇ ṇilaviṉ payantuyttum
Kaṇṇataiiya kaṭaikkankuḷān

Turaimukam

Mā akāviri maṇamkūṭum
Tūuekkart tuyilmaṭintu
Vāliṇar maṭaltāḻai
Velāḻi viyanteruvil
Nalliraivan porulkākkum
Tollisai toḻilmākkaḷ
Kāyçinatta katirçcelvan
Therpoonṭa māapōla

Port State of Custom-Collectors (116-125)

To guard treasures of the goodly king
Are men to the call of ancient task
Who labour forth bereft of falter collecting toll.
They liken horses that the scorching Sun's
Chariot draw each day long; devoid of   (140)
Rest and failure do they customs levy
In the street of width and breadth
Abutting the beachy sea with bunches of
Whitish florets and sheathed pines.
Sleeping scarce but repose do take they   (145)
On wavy sands of splendorous fragrance
The great *Kāviri* brings forth with diverse blooms.

Warehouse Courtyard (126-141)

In the warehouse, huge and are piled
Imports from sea and to it experts pass from land;
Both these smack of times of monsoon rains   (150)
When clouds that from sea water draw and from
Mountains in torrents shower which to the sea fluvial go.
Arrive assorted goods, unmeasured and limitless
To the warehouse vast where strongmen
On vigilant guard stamp the tiger mark,   (155)
And thus the goods passage easy find and
Reach out to the courtyard and amassing in heaps
Over which hounds and goats in jumpy play indulge

வைகல்தொறும் அசைவின்றி
125 உலகுசெயக் குறைபடாது
வான்முகந்தநீர் மலைப்பொழியவும்
மலைப்பொழிந்தநீர் கடல்பரப்பவும்
மாரிபெய்யும் பருவம்போல
நீர்நின்று நிலத்தேற்றவும்
130 நிலத்தினின்று நீர்ப்பரப்பவும்
அளந்தறியாப் பலபண்டம்
வரம் பறியாமை வந்தீண்டி
அருங்கடிப் பெருங்காப்பின்
வலியுடை வல்லணங்கினோன்
135 புலிபொறித்துப் புறம்போக்கி
மதிநிறைந்த மலிபண்டம்
பொதிமூடைப் போர் ஏறி
மழையாடு சிமைய மால்வரைக் கவாஅன்
வரையாடு வருடைத் தோற்றம்
140 கூருகிர் ஞமலிக் கொடுந்தாள் ஏற்றை

Vaikaltorum asaivin_ri
Ulkuceyak kuraipaṭātu
Vānmukantanīr malaippo_liyavum
Malaippolintanīr kaṭalparappavum
Māripeyyum paruvampōla
Nīrinin_ru nilatteṭravum
Nilattinininru nīrparappavum
A_l antariyāp palapanṭam
Varam pa_riyāmai vantīnti
Arunkaṭip peruṅkāppin
Valiyutai vallananki_nōn
Puliporittup purampōkki
Mati_nirain_ta malipanṭam
Potimūṭaip pōr e_ri
Ma_laiyoṭu simaiya malvaraik kavāa_n
Varaiyaṭu varuṭ ait tōṭ ram pōlak
Kūrukir ñamalik koṭuntā_l ētrai

With their clawed nails and flexural legs
Bearing semblance to stags that play on   (160)
Mountain tops and slopes where clouds vapoury gather
And verdant bamboos long and strong abound.

Comely Maidens and Merchant Streets (142-158)

In palatial houses built with shutting steps

There are pials around with ladders leaned,
And chambers many with ingress big and small   (165)
And corridors long; high on terrace of storeys
Tall of reach for clouds, maidens fair of feet
And fleshly thighs that to each dear remain,
Of broad and shapely hips, and sport of bijouterie,
Clad in raiment thin on coral skin,   (170)
With cervine looks and pavonine stance
And pisttacine speech and of slender form
Lean on windows that passage to breeze provide;
Palms closed, they fold their hands in worship stance
That semblance bear to floret sprouts of *Kāntal*   (175)
Which nectar thin secrete on mountains high;
Festive days this place continual does have
Lord *Murukā* to honour; frenzied women dance
Whose rhythm hornets, lutes and drums consonance keep;
Such a reveling ceaseless goes
In market streets long and wide.   (180)

ஏழகத் தகரொடுஉகளும் முன்றில்

வளிநுழையும் வாய்பொருந்தி
ஓங்குவரைமருங்கின் நுண்தாதுஉறைக்கும்
காந்தளம் துடுப்பின் கவிகுலைஅன்ன
செறிதொடிமுன்கை கூப்பிச் செவ்வேள்
155 வெறியாடும் மகளிரொடுசெறியத்தாஅய்க்

ஆவணவீதிகள்

குறுந்தொடைநெடும்படிக்கால்
கொடுந்திண்ணைப் பல்தகைப்பில்
புழைவாயில் போகிடைகழி
145 மழைதோயும் உயர்மாடத்துச்
சேவடிச் செறிகுறங்கின்
பாசிழைப் பகட்டல்குல்
தூசுடைத் துகிர்மேனி
மயிலியல் மான்நோக்கின்
150 கிளிமழலைமென்சாயலோர்

Eḻakattakaroṭuukaḷummunril

Āavaṇa Vītikaḷ

Kuruntoṭai neṭumpaṭikkāl
Koṭuntiṇṇaip paltakaippil
Puḻaivāyil pōkiṭaikaḻi
Maḻaitōyum uyarmāṭatuc
Cēvaṭic cerikuṟaṅkin
Pāsiḻaip pakaṭṭalkul
Tūsuṭait tukirmēṇi
Mayiliyal mānnōkkin
Kiḷimaḻalai mensāyalōr
Vaḷinuḻaiyum Vāyporunti
Ōṅkuvarai maruṅkin nuṇṭātu uṟaikkum
Kāntalam tuṭupin kavikulaianna
Ceritoṭi munkai kūppic cevvēḷ
Veriyaṭum makaḷiroṭu ceriyat tāaiyk

Diverse Flags Hoisted (159-183)

In the temples of blemishless Gods invoked
The holy ingresses with flowers are bedecked;

There flaunt flags for many to oblate,
Foisted on the roof of shields that rest on spears
Firmed on ground greased with cow's dung dissolved;
There flutters a flag of cloth of white,   (185)
Brighteous as blooms of sugarcances graceful stand
On banks of silver sands brought on
By the fluvial jungle stream; likens these blooms
Rice strewn as offering on viands rich and delicate

(190)

To the brim of baskets and those on cloth-sheets

spread.

There foisted and hovers yet another flag,
Smacks that of didactics to disputes redress
By savants and scholars erudite and speckless
With tradition rich to reverence infuse   (195)
In those that are of wisdom scarce;
In the port of wavy sea of *Pukār*
There flaunt diverse flags on masts of ships
That do resemblance bear to elephant bulls
That the pegs they are tied to shake.   (200)
The courtyard brims with bustle where meat
Of fish is cut and sliced and fried;

குழல் அகவயாழ்முரல
முழவதிர முரசியம்ப
விழவறாவியல் ஆவணத்து

பல்வகைக் கொடிகள்

மையறுசிறப்பின் தெய்வம் சேர்ததிய
160 மலரணிவாயில் பலர்தொழு கொடியும்
வருபுனல் தந்த வெண்மனல் கான்யாற் (று)
உருகெழு கரும்பின் ஒண்பூப் போலக்
கூழுடைக் கொழுமஞ்சிகைத்
தாழுடைத் தண்பணியத்து
165 வாலரிசிப் பலிசிதறிப்
பாகுகுத்த பசுமெழுக்கில்
காழ்ஊன்றியகவிகிடுகின்
மேல்ஊன்றிய துகில்கொடியும்
பல்கேள்வித் துறைபோகிய
170 தொல்லாணை நல்லாசிரியர்
உறழ்குறித் தெடுத்த உருகெழுகொடியும்

Kuḻalakavayālmurala
Muḻavatiramuraciympa
Viḻavarāviyalāvaṇattu

PalvakaiKoṭikaḷ

Maiyaṟu ciṟappiṉ teivam cērttiya
Malaraṇi Vāyilpalartoḻukoṭiyum
Varupuṉal tanta veṇmaṉal kāṉyāṭ (ru)
Urukeḻu karumpiṉ oṇpūp pōlak
Kūḻuṭaik koḻumancikait
Tāḻutait tāṉpaṇiyattu
Vālaricip palicitarip
Pākukata pacumeḻukkil
Kāḻūnṟiya Kavikiṭukin
Mēlūnṟiya tukilkoṭiyum
Palkēḷivit turaipōkiya
Tollāṇai nallāciriyar
Uraḻkurit teṭutta urukeḻu kotiyum

At the entrance of toddy shops, flowers
In offering to Gods are strewn on heaps of sand.
There the flag that marks of sale wafts   (205)
Along with flags of diverse tones and shapes rich;
Shades of these defiance pose unto
Rays of sun that can scarcely pass and these
The wealth and opulence of *Pukār* tell.

Wealth of Varied Kinds (184-193)

As goodly angels watchful guard eternal keep,   (210)
Permeates the street broad of the city port with
Wealth of varied sorts that blend enchanting make.
Romping horses brought on sea from alien lands
And bundles of pepper black from domestic domain,
Sparkling gems and gold from the Himalayan
                                        Mounts; (215)
Of the western ghats from *Kutaku* eagle-wood
And sandal; pearls and corals from seas
Southward and eastern, and diverse things
Grown on beds of the Ganges and *Kāviri*
Foods of import from the Lankan land, and   (220)
Goods for joyful use from the Kaṭaram country

Together with things rare and big of size
Gather in weighty heap on land, it to pliable make.

வெளில் இளக்கும் களிறுபோலத்
தீம்புகார்த் திரைமுன்துறைத்
தூங்குநாவாய் துவன்றிருக்கை
175   மிசைக்கூம்பின் நசைக்கொடியும்
மீன்தடிந்து விடக்கறுத்து
ஊன்பொரிக்கு ஒலிமுன்றில்
மணல்குலைஇ மலர்சிதறிப்
பலர்புகுமனைப் பலிப்புதலின்
180   நறவுநொடைக் கொடியோடு
பிறபிறவும் நளிவிரைஇப்
பல்வேறுருவின் பதாகை நீழல்
செல்கதிர் நுழையாச் செழுநகர் வரைப்பின்

வளந்தலை மயங்கிய மறுகு

செல்லா நல்லிசை அமரர் காப்பின்
185   நீரீன் வந்த நிமிர்பாப் புரவியும்
காலின் வந்த கரங்கறி மூடையும்
வடமலைப் பிறந்த மணியும் பொன்னும்

Veḻil iḻakkum kalirupōlat
Tīmpukārt tiraimuṉṯuṟait
Tūṅkuṉāvāy tuvaṉrirukkai
Misaikkūmpiṉ ṉacaikkoṭiyum
Mīntaṭiṉtu Vitakkaruttu
Ūṉporikkum olimuṉril
Maṇal Kuvaii malarcitarip
Palarpukumaṉaip palipputaviṉ
Ṉaravuṉaṭaik kotiyōṭu
Pirapiravum ṉaṉiviraiip
Palvē ruruviṉ patākai ṉī ḻal
Celkatir nuḻaiyac ceḻunakar varaippiṉ

Vaḷantalai Mayaṅkia Maṟuku

Cellā nallisai amarar kāppin
Nīriṉ vanta nimirparip puraviyum
Kaliṉvanta karaṅkaṟi mūtaiyum
Vaṭamalaip piṟanta maṇ iyum poṉṉum

Grandeur of Peasants (194-205)

Along the stretch of sea and land
In courtyards of houses and humble huts   (225)
Of fishfolk and butchers free of pursuit professional,
The piscine,bovine and capric stock leap in joy
And in slumber seal and further their breed indeed.
The peasants that with love their job do.
With curvy plough do unto others succour

                                        extend, (230)
And thus deter not from their moral stand.
They from murderers their vicious intent dispel,
And from thieves their vile thievery efface,
And unto Gods hymns chant and worship make,
And oblation offer in sacramental fire,   (235)
Guard cows and bullocks, and spread the fame
Of those ingrained stand in *Vetas* four.,
Treat guests with viands and victuals delightful
And offer food afresh to beggars poor.

குடமலைப் பிறந்த ஆரமும் அகிலும்
தென்கடல் முத்தும் குணகடல் துகிரும்
190 கங்கை வாரியும் காவிரிப் பயனும்
ஈழத் துணவும் காழகத் தாக்கமும்
அரியவும் பெரியவும் நெறியாண்டி
வளந்தலை மயங்கிய நனந்தலை மறுகின்

உழவர் குடிச்சிறப்பு

நீர்நாப் பண்ணும் நிலத்தின் மேலும்
195 ஏமாப்ப இனிதுதுஞ்சிக்
கிளைகலித்துப் பகைபேனாது
வலைஞர் முன்றில் மீன்பிறழவும்
விலைஞர் குரம்பை மாஈண்டவும்
கொலைகடிந்தும் களவு நீக்கியும்
200 அமரர்ப் பேணியும் ஆவுதி அருத்தியும்
நல்லானொடு பகடோம்பியும்
நான்மறையோர் புகழ்பரப்பியும்
பண்ணியம் அட்டியும் பசும்பதம் கொடுத்தும்

Kutamalaip piṟanta āramum akilum
Teṉkaṭal muttum kuṇakaṭal tukirum
Kaṅkai vārium kāvirip payaṉum
Īḻattuṇavum kāḻakattākkamum
Ariyavum periyavum ṉeriya īṉṭi
Vaḷantalai mayaṅkiya naṉantalai marukiṉ

Uḷavar Kuṭiciṟappu

Nīrnāp paṇṇum nilattiṉ mēlum
Ēmāppa iṉitutuñcik
Kiḷaikalittup pakaipēṉatu
Valaiñar muṉṟil mīṉpiṟaḷavum
Vilaiñar kurambai mā īṇṭavum
Kolaikaṭintum kaḷavu nī kkiyum
Amararp pēṇiyum āvuti arutiyum
Nallāṉoṭu pakaṭōmpiyum
Nāṉmaṟaiyōr pukaḷparappiyum
Paṇṇiyam aṭṭiyum pacumpatam koṭutum

Grandeur of Merchants (206-212)

Good hearted merchants of ancient wealth   (240)
Like the central nail to the lengthy yoke,
Stand just, dreading destiny of descendents
Voice the truth and barter goods in balance perfect,
Tell out in open the income thereon
And live in clustered assemblage there in *Pukār*. (245)
With blend of mind and love and joy.

Outlanders Live in Harmony (213-217)

Like the goodly kins of varied wits
Visiting distant lands and in friendship move
With varied folk that in gaiety throng and
Festive occasion make in heritage place ancient,
The town of *Pukār* pulsates with   (250)
Immigrants versed well in tongues
Of countries blemishless and in consonance live
With blend of mind and love and joy in harmony sweet.

Crux of the Song (218-220)

Were I even to get the city deterred not
In grace and fame, I shall not part   (255)
From my lady-love with hairs long and dark
And jewelled in glitter. Long live, Oh! My inner self.

புண்ணியம் முட்டாத் தண்ணிழல் வாழ்க்கைக்
205   கொடுமேழி நசைஉழவர்

வணிகர் குடிச் சிறப்பு

நெடுநுகத்துப் பகல்போல
நடுவுநின்ற நன்னெஞ்சினோர்
வடுவஞ்சி வாய்மொழிந்து
தமவும் பிறவும் ஒப்பநாடிக்
210   கொள்வதூஉம் மிகைகொளாது கொடுப்பதூஉம்
                குறைகொடாது
பல்பண்டம் பகர்ந்துவீசும்
தொல்கொண்டித் துவன்றிருக்கைப்

புலம் பெயர் மாக்கள்

பல்லாயமொடு பதிபழகி
வேறுவேறுயர்ந்த முதுவாய் ஒக்கல்
215   சாறயர் மூதூர் செயன்றுதொக் காங்கு
மொழிபல பெருகிய பழிதீர் தேஅத்துப்
புலம்பெயர் மாக்கள் கலந்தினி துறையும்

Puṇṇiyammuṭṭattaṇ ṇ iḻalVāḻkkaik
Koṭ umēḻinacaiuḻavar

Vaṇikar Kuṭi Cirappu

Neṭunuḵattup pakalpōla
Natuvuniṉṟa naṉṉeñciṉōr
Vaṭuvanci Vāymoḻintu
Tamavum piṟavum oppanāṭik
Koḷvatūum mikaikoḷatuKoṭuppatūum Kuṟaikeṭatu
Palpaṇṭam pakarntuvīcum
Tolkoṇṭit tuvaṉṟirukkaip

Pulam Peyar Mākkaḷ

Pallāyamotu patipalaki
Vēruvēruyarnta mutuvāy okkal
Sārayar mūtūr ceṉṟutok kaṅku
Moḻipala perukiya paḻtīr tēettup
Pulampeyar mākkaḷ kalantini tuṟaiyum

Tirumavalavan's Ascendance to the Throne (221-227)

Just as the tigrine cub grows with edgy claws
And wavy stripes despite in cage immured
Valava<u>n</u>Tiruma̅ in fiendish guard cabined   (260)
Which in turn his valour nursed and sagacity whetted;
The secure walls strong and close he surmounts
And gains the uneasy crown by righteous means
Like the elephant bull with a lengthy trunk
Goring to naught the pit walls of the pitfall   (265)
With its tusks sharp and sturdy freeing
Itself and to its mate access gains.

Karika̅la<u>n</u>'s War of Plunder (228-239)

Joyous not with his crown and right to rule retrieved,
Loving warfare *Valava<u>n</u>Tiruma̅* surged ahead
With elephants of majestic grace that with feet of nails (270)
Plundered the forts of foes that were sentinel strong,
With their tusks sturdy, and broke their gates
And rolled the heads of hostile kings with diadem firm.
With these along, steeds decked with chiselled beads,
And *Valavan* himself sporting blooms of varied *Pu̅lai*   (275)
Sembling a mound densed with vines and shrubs
                                        and thickets
Went to the war-camp spacious that had a mammoth
                                        drum.

பாட்டின் உரிப்பொருள்

முட்டாச் சிறப்பிற் பட்டினம் பெறினும்
வாரிருங் கூந்தல் வயங்கிழையொழிய
220 வாரேன் வாழியநெஞ்சே! கூருகிர்க்

திருமாவளவனின் பெருமைகள்

திருமாவளவன் தாயம் எய்தல்

கொடுவரிக் குருளை கூட்டுள் வளர்ந்தாங்குப்
பிறர் பிணியகத்திருந்து பீடுகாழ் முற்றி
அருங்கரைஅவியக் குத்திக் குழிகொன்று
பெருங்கை யானைபிடிபுக் காங்கு
225 நுண்ணிதின் உணர நாடி நண்ணார்
செறிவுடைத் திணகாப் பேறிவாள் கழித்(து)
உருகெழுதாயம் ஊழின் எய்தி

Pāṭṭin Uripporuḷ

Muttaccirappir pattiṉam periṉum
Vārirum kūntalvayaṅkiḻai yoḻiya
Vārēṉ vāḻiyaneñcē! Kurukir

TirumāVaḷ avaniṉ Perumaikaḷ
Tirumāvaḷavaṉ Tāyam Eital

Koṭuvarik kuruḷai kūṭṭuḷ Vaḷarntaṉkup
Piṟar, piṉiyakattiruntu pīṭukaḷ mutṟi
Aruṅkarai aviyak kuttik kuḻikoṉṟu
Peruṅkai yāṉaipiṭipuk kāṅku
Nuṇṇitiṉ uṇara nā ṭi naṉṉār
Cerivutait tiṇkāp perivaḷ Kaḻit(tu)
Urukeḻutāyam ūḻiṉ eiti

திருமாவளவனின் உழிஞைப் போர்

பெற்றவை மகிழ்தல் செய்யான் செற்றோர்
கடிஅரண் தொலைத்த கதவுகொல் மருப்பின்
230 முடியுடைக் கருந்தலை புரட்டும் முன்தாள்

TirumāVaḷavaniṉ Uḻiñaippōr

Petṟavai makiḻtal ceyyāṉ cetṟōr
Kaṭi araṉ tolaitta katavukol maruppiṉ
Muṭiyuṭaik karuṉtalai puraṭṭum muṉtāḷ

Guarded well was the roaring drum and its
Beating-strip demon's eye resemblance bore,
And unto the enemy's front *Valava<u>n</u>* went,   (280)
Them he trounced to naught that set eagles hover
In sky vast to prey upon bodies dead,
And victories gained and content not with this lot
In wrathful surge he moved further on to
Arable lands and the people therein he migrants
made. (285)

Destruction of Arable Lands of Foes (240-245)

There in these fecund lands once abounded
Sugary canes with whitish blooms and paddy rich;
Lilies of sorts both *Kuvaḷai* and *Neital,*
With each other braided and blended grew.
The wider tanks wherein former times   (290)
Gavials roistered, now give a piteous scene
Where *Aruku* with fatty roots, and sedges grow;
The lands and tanks now are dry of water
Where bucks with ribbed horns and hinds
Do leap about and play.

Destruction of Temple (246-251)

The consorts of hostile kings taken captives once   (295)
Wont to dip in tanks meant for drinks,
And lightened lamps at dusk that lasting went

உகிருடை யடிய ஓங்கெழில் யானை
வடிமணிப் புரவியொடுவயவர் வீழப்
பெருநல் வானத்துப் பருந்துலாய் நடப்பத்
தூறிவர் துறுகற் போலப் போர்வேட்டு
235   வேறுபல் பூளையோ டுழிஞைசு சூடிப்
பேய்க்கண் அன்ன பிளிறுகடி முரசம்
மாக்கண் அகலறை அதிர்வன முழங்க
முனைகெடச் சென்று முன்சமம் முருக்கித்
தலைதவச் சென்று தண்பணை எடுப்பி

பகைவர் மருதநிலங்களை அழித்தல்

240   வெண்பூக் கரும்பொடு செந்நெல் நீடி
மாயிதழக் குவளையொடு நெய்தலும் மயங்கிக்
கராஅங் கலித்த கண்ணகன் பொய்கைக்
கொழுங்காற் புதவமொடு செருந்தி நீடிச்
செறுவும் வாவியு மயங்கி நீரற்று
245   அறுகோட் டிரலையொடு மான்பிணை உகளவும்

Ukiruṭai aṭiya ōṅkeḻil yāṉai
Vaṭimaṇip puraviyoṭu vayavar vīḻap
Peruṉal vāṉattup paruntulāi ṉaṭappat
Tūrivar turukal pōlap pōrveṭṭu
Vērupal pūlaiyō ṭuuliñai cūṭip
Pēykkaṇ anna piḷirukaṭi muracam
Mākkaṇ akalarai atirvana muḻaṅka
Munaikeṭac ceṉru muṉsamam muṟukkit
Talaitavac ceṉrutaṉpaṇai eṭuppi

Pakaivar MarutaNilaṅkalai Aḻittal

Veṇpūk karumpoṭu ceṉṉel nīti
Māyitaḻk kuvaḷaiyoṭu neytalum mayaṅkik
Karā aṅk kalittakaṇṇakan poykaik
Koḻuṅkāṉputavamoṭu cerunti nīṭic
Ceṟuvum Vāviyu mayṅki nīraṟṟu
Arukōṭṭ iralaiyoṭu māṉpiṇai ukaḷavum

In the smeared sanctum with flowers decked
Stayed aliens and natives and worship offered
Unto the sanctified God invoked in stone installed;   (300)
The temple thus lodging unto outlanders did provide.
There as of now elephant bulls strong and splendid
Along with their mates rest and repose seek,
And against pillars strong and tall they lean
And rub and them they render frail.   (305)

Destruction of Concert Halls (252-260)

The streets strewn with fragrant and priceless
Blooms rare and throbbed with rubato of majestic
Beats on snare drums by spirited maestros that went
With tunes sweet emerging deft and 'lightful
From the lyre with strings tense and taut   (310)
And where teemed festivals, now barrenness pervades
With fear coupled; and there prevail in abundance
Dense tiny florets of *Cow's* thorn along with *Aruku* grass.
Skulk of foxes mouthed wide give out fearsome howl
And with weeping hoots of stare of barn owls,   (315)
The sedge of bitterns yelp, and with the crowd
Of wraiths male in form the female ravenants
Company make with tuft of hair that fall and trail.

அம்பல அழிவு

கொண்டி மகளிர் உண்டுறை மூழ்கி
அந்தி மாட்டிய நந்தாவிளக்கின்
மலரணி மெழுக்கம் ஏறிப் பலர்தோழ
வம்பலர் சேக்கம் கந்துடைப் பொதியில்
250 பருநிலை நெடுந்தூண் ஒல்கத் தீண்டிப்
பெருநல் யானையொடு பிடிபுணர்ந் துறையவும்

மன்றங்கள் பாழ்பட்டமை

அருவிலை நறும்பூத் தூஉய்த் தெருவின்
முதுவாய்க் கோடியர் முழவொடு புணர்ந்த
திரிபுரி நரம்பின் தீந்தொடை யோர்க்கும்
255 பெருவிழாக் கழிந்த பேஎமுதிர் மன்றத்துச்
சிறுபூ நெருஞ்சியொ டறுகை பம்பி
அழல்வாய் யோரிஅஞ்சுவரக் கதிர்ப்பவும்
அழுகுரற் கூகையோ டாண்டலை விளிப்பவும்
கணங்கொள் கூளியொடு கதுப்பிகுத் தசைஇப்
260 பிணந்தின் யாக்கைப் பேய்மகள் துவன்றவும்

Ampala Alivu

Koṇṭi makaḷir uṇṭurai mūḻki
Anti māṭṭiya nantāviḷakkiṉ
Malaraṇi meḻukkamērip palartoḻa
Vampalar cēkkam Kaṇṭuṭaip potiyil
Parunilai neṭuntūṉ olkat tīṇṭip
Perunal yaṉaiyoṭu piṭipuṇarn turiayavum

Maṉṟaṅkal Pāḻpaṭṭamai

Aruvilai ṉarumpūt tū uyt teruviṉ
Mutuvaik kōtiyar muḻavoṭu puṇarnta
Tiripuri ṉarampiṉ tīntoṭai ōrkkum
Peruviḻāk kaḻinta pēemutir maṉṟattuc
Cirupū ṉeruñiyo ṭarukai pampi
Aḻalvā yori añuvarak katirppavum
Aḻukurar kūkaiyoṭu āṇṭalai viḷippavum
Kaṇaṅkol kūḻiyoṭu katupikut tasaiip
Piṇ antiṉ yākkaip pēymakaḷ tuvaṉravum

Destruction of Towns of Foes (261-268)

At the ingress of mansions where pillars   (320)
Round and shapely stood, guests would ceaseless
Come and feed; the place had kitchens with
Heaps and mounds of viands that never inadequate
went,
And where stood goodly houses painted rich and bright
That thrived with milky wealth and babbling
parrots, (325)
Hunters footing leathern gaiter thronged holding
Vicious bows and to the beats of tenor drums rubbed
Granaries rich that now improverished stand
wherefrom
During daylight curvy-beaked barn owls hoot.

Valavan Tiruma's Prowess of Resolve (269-273)

Thus marched forward the King of fury   (330)
Gratified not with spoils wrought on
Walls guarded secure and countries gorgeous
Of foes whom he routed clean of stock
To the thought of mass 'bout his prowess
That he would mountains dislodge and   (335)
Would all the seas drain, and drag
Down the sky, and still and maim the air
And could all his intent flawless render.

பகைவர் நகரங்கள் பாழ்பட்டமை

கொடுங்கால் மாடத்து நெடுக்கடைத் துவன்றி
விருந்துண்டு ஆனாப் பெருஞ்சோற் றட்டில்
ஒண்சுவர் நல்லில் உயர்திணை இருந்து
பைங்கிளி மிழற்றம் பாலார் செழுநகர்த்
265 தொடுதோல் அடியர் துடிபடக் குழீஇக்
கொடுவில் எயினர் கொள்ளை யுண்ட
உணவில் வறுங்கூட் டுள்ளகத் திருந்து
வளைவாய்க் கூகை நன்பகல் குழறவும்

திருமாவனவனின் கருதியது முடிக்கும் திறம்

அருங்கடி வரைப்பின் ஊர்கவின் அழியப்
270 பெரும்பாழ் செய்தும் அமையான் மருங்கற
மலையகழ்க் குவனே கடல்தூர்க் குவனே
வான்வீழ்க் குவனே வளிமாற் றுவன்எனத்
தான்முன்னிய துறைபோகலின்

திருமாவனவனின் வெற்றிகள்

பல்ஒளியர் பணிபொடுங்கத்

Pakaivar Ṉakaraṅkai Pā̱lpattamai

Koṭuṅkā̱l mā̱ṭattu neṭuṅ katait tuva̱ṉri
Viruntuntu ā̱ṉā̱p peruñcō̱t ṟattil
Oṉcuvar nallil uyartiṉai iruṇtu
Paiṅkili mi̱la̱ṯrum pā̱lā̱r ce̱luṉakart
Toṭutō̱l aṭiyar tuṭipatak ku̱l̠iik
Koṭuvil eyi̱ṉar ko̱l̠l̠ai yuṇta
U̱ṉavil va̱ruṅkuṭ ṭu̱l̠l̠akat tiruntu
Va̱l̠aivā̱yk kū̱kai ̱ṉaṉpakal ku̱l̠a̱ravum

Tirumavaḷava̱ṉi̱ṉ Karutiyatu Muṭikkum Ti̱ram

Arunkaṭi varaippi̱ṉ ū̱rkavi̱ṉ a̱l̠iyap
Perumpa̱l̠ ceytum amaiyā̱ṉ marunkara
Malaiyaka̱lk kuvaṉē̱ kataltū̱rk kuvaṉē̱
Vā̱nvī̱ l̠k kuvanē̱ va̱l̠imā̱t ̱ruvanenat
Tā̱ṉmu̱ṉṉiya tu̱raipō̱kali̱ṉ

Tirumavalavanin Vetrikal

Palo̱l̠iyar paṇipotuṅkat
They do dance with gusto, and corpses guzzle.

ValavanTiruma's Victories (274-282)

His fiery ire and pride in perfect blend unite
In seizing ramparts firm and strong of deadly
                                    foes;   (340)
His resolve valiant and massive army,
Inherent courage and glance of fury
Cast at rivals make them bend in shame;
And with awesome fear subdue; dexterous in
Diverse fields those of ancient *Aruva* land beg
                                    of him   (345)

For command to abide, while the northern kings
Fade and wither; the western kings go bereft of
Psychic strength while the valour of *Pāntiyan*
Finds its spoils; the shepherd kings stand helpless
With lineage blighted, and occurs there   (350)
The disastrous rout of *Irunkovel's* kin.

Formative Works of Tiruma Valavan (283-292)

Woodlands he destroys for habitations to thrive,
Digs ponds and tanks to richness extend;
Expands city *Urantai* that with topless mansions
                                    prevail
With massive doors, rules temples and citizens (355)
And stability unto them unfaltering provides.
Portals big and small unto the city he devises,
And fills battlements with quivers in locks and stocks;

275 தொல் அருவாளர் தொழில் கேட்ப
வடவர் வாடக் குடவர் கூம்பத்
தென்னவன் திறல்கெடச் சீறி மன்னர்
மன்எயில் கதுவும் மதனுடை நோன்தாள்
மாத்தானை மறமொய்ம்பின்
280 செங்கண்ணால் செயிர்த்து நோக்கிப்
புன்பொதுவர் வழிபொன்ற
இருங்கோவேள் மருங்குசாய

ஆக்கப் பணிகள்

காடுகொன்று நாடாக்கிக்
குளம்தொட்டு வளம்பெருக்கிப
285 பிறங்குநிலை மாடத்து உறந்தை போக்கிக்
கோயிலோடு குடி நிறீஇ
வாயிலொடு புழையமைத்து
ஞாயில்தொறும் புதை நிறீஇப்
பொருவெம் எனப் பெயர்கொடுத்து
290 ஒருவேம் எனப் புறக்கொடாது.

Tolaruvaḷar toḻikeṭpa
Vaṭavar vāṭak kuṭavar kūmpat
Thennavan tiralkeṭac cīri mannar
Maṇeyil katuvum matanuṭai nōntāḷ
Māttānai maramoympin
Ceṅkaṇṇāl ceyirttū nōkkip
Punpotuvar Valiponra
Iruṅkōvēl marunkucāya

Ākkap Paṇikaḷ

Kāṭukonru nāṭakkik
Kuḷamtoṭṭu vaḷamperukkip
Piṟaṅ kunilai māṭutu urantai pōkkik
Kōyiloṭu kuṭinirīi
Vāyilotu puḻaiyamaittu
Ñayiltorum putainirīip
Poruvōm enap peyarkoṭuttu
Oruvēm enap purakkoṭatu

With yelling-resolve to fight steadfast against foes
Thereby goading warriors to falter not in fight; (360)
All these make his walls stable and valiant
That stand radiant here the spirit of
Triumph pervades ever.

Tiruma Valavan's Blissful Life (293-299)

Those kings with drums of tightened tymphan
Who have before *Tirumā* hitherto not bent
Now bereft of glory stand and unto him obeissance
pay. (365)
The beads of green on their crowns rub
Against his legs strong and shapely which anklets
grace;
Frequent hugs he receives from his urchins
Who hither and thither run wearing bangles gold,
And his consort decked in bijoutrie rich   (370)
Touches his chest with her lotus-buddy breasts,
The paste of sandal red smeared thereon
Chafed goes; worn in dazzling jewelry he with valiance
Suffers the foes and the lion he semblance bears.

The Song's Rightful Concept (293-301)

The woods I have to pass are wilder   (375)
Than the spear that *Tirumā* on his foes targets;
Her shoulders broad and tender are far more
Cooler than His Sceptre's justly rule.   (378)

திருநிலைஇய பெருமன்எயில்
மின் ஒளி எறிப்பத் தம்ஒளி மழுங்கி

இன்பச் சிறப்பு

விசிபிணி முழவின் வேந்தர் சூடிய
பசுமணி பொருத பரேர் எறுழ்க் கழற்கால்
295 பொற்றொடிப் புதல்வர் ஓடி ஆடவும்
முற்றிழை மகளிர் முகிழ்முலை திளைப்பவும்
செஞ்சாந்து சிதைந்த மார்பின் ஒண்பூண்
அரிமா அன்ன அணங்குடைத் துப்பின்

பாட்டின் உரிப்பொருள்

திருமா வளவன் தெவ்வர்க்கு ஒக்கிய
300 வேலினும் வெய்ய கானம் அவன்
கோவினும் தண்ணிய தடமென் தோளே.

Tirunailaiiya perumaṉeyil
Miṉ oḷi erippaaat tamoli maḻuṅki

Inpac Ciṟappu

Vicipiṇi muḻaviṉ Vēntar cūṭiya
Pasumaṇi poruta parēr eruḻk kaḷarkāl
Potṟoṭip puṭalvar ōṭi aṭavum
Mutṟiḻai makaḷir mukiḻmulai tiḷaipaavum
Ceñcāntu citainta mārpiṉ oṇpūṇ
Arima anna aṇ aṅkuṭait tuppin

Pāttiṉ Uripporuḷ

Tiruma Valavan tevvarkku okkiya
Vēliṉum veeya kāṉam avam
Kōliṉum taṇṇ iya taṭameṉ tōḷe.

NOTES

1-7   The river *Kaviri* was unfailing in the days of yore. Always flourishingly fluvial, the river originating in the *Kutaku* mountain (now in *Karnataka*) never went dry. It contributed to agricultural prosperity and thereby to material wealth. The poet heightens this aspect of the river saying that even if Venus, the sparkling star were to change its course and go southward, the *Kaviri* would never betray the people. Thus, at the outset the magnificence of the river is highlighted.

8-20   The description pertains to agricultural wealth of the *Cōla* state. Despite the region being *Neital* (sea and its shore), it has lands which is a commonalty with all regions. The lands which stretch far and wide never fail in their yield. The rural scene is familiar with boiling of sugarcane juice from which country sugar (jaggery) is prepared. The smoke that emanates in the process withers the flowers that stand blooming along. The region abounds in *Neital* flowers – a variety of lily. Even buffaloes feed on paddy, a sign of richness of the region. The calves of buffaloes sleep on heaps of paddy. Coconut trees, banana plants and areca palms yield their fruits in clusters. There is aboundant growth of turmeric, kyle, (sēmpu), and ginger.

L 12   *Neital* – Indian Water Lily

L 17   *areca* palm – a plant, a slender and tall tree the fruits of which are processed and used along with betel leaves in chewing.

L 20   *rhizome, kyle or arum* (*sēmpu* in **Tamil**) which is a root, both round and oval shaped. Usually this is boiled in pulse porridge called Sambar, or fried added with curry powder, and spiced with frittered mustard and green or red chillies in oil.

21-28   These lines describe the picture of village life, the purpose being to draw the reader's attention to the richness that abounds there. Houses in villages around *Kaviri Pumpattinam* have expansive courtyards. In these courtyards stand beautiful maidens both innocent and radiant. They wear earrings made of solid gold. When domestic fowls come to feed on paddy piled up or spread for drying, these women huri their earrings to chase them away. But these ornaments roll and block the passage of tri-wheeled chariots pushed and played with by unchins who also wear jewellery in the form of anklets in gold. Life among diverse tribes in villages abutting each other is harmonious bereft of rancour.

31-43   The town is also referred to as *Pukār*. The place abounds in groves. The trunks of trees are used to tie the boats which are strong. These boats go loaded with whitish salt and return carrying paddy in lieu. The tied boats look like horses tied in stables in an orderly way. The flowery gardens bordering the groves earn money by their blooms which is a matter of pride to the people of the place. There is a tank which looks like the Moon particularly when it prevails juxtaposed with the constellation called *Maham*. Apart from this, there are two lakes. And dipping for a bath there, according to the belief of people, would bring them sensual pleasure both in this life and the life beyond this birth.

L 39   *Maham.* A star in the sky known for its beautiful shape to which is compared the lofty bank of the tank. The tank is further compared to the Moon when it dazzles in clear sky free of rain-bearing clouds.

44-55   The gusto of people in general to have qualitative life both in this birth and in the world after death is revealed here. One of the customs to earn tributes in this birth and virtues for sustenance in the other world is to feed the mass. The citizens of *Pukār* are famous for maintaining kitchens which are busy throughout the day.
The town has very strong walls wherein one can find the emblazonry of the Tiger's image – the symbol of the *Cōla* kingdom. The walls drum out the pride of the land As the kitchens are always busy boiling rice and other viands to offer unto people of all sorts, there flows perpetually porridge-like paste which runs down to the streets. Bullocks which come to drink this discharge clash against one another and the streets are made slushy. They dry up soon. And when chariots pass the way, the dried up slush rises as dust. The palace of the kind which is white with its diverse paintings outside looks like an elephant smeared with slush in designs.

56-68   The poet resorts to describing other places, not covered by earlier passages. There abound in *Pukār,* ponds with cooler reserve of water. There prevail many yards to provide hay to bullocks and other cattle. Cloisters accommodate hermits and saints who with their many locks of hair do indulge in penance. They kindle sacramental fire and offer oblations to Gods. Diverse things are offered in fire as oblation and the smoke emanating is a menace to Cuckoos living in trees. They detest this smoke and fly away in pairs. They do partake of the resting place of Pigeons in distant groves verdant in growth. The place is well guarded by demons and passage into that place is very hard.

69-85   In *Pukār* there is an exclusive ground where soldiers practise the game of war. They are all characterised by pride and valiance. They eat roasted shrimp and boiled crab meat, sport *Atumpu* flowers which are to be found creeping on parched ground and *Āmpal* blooms that grow flourishingly along the river banks. Those who have gathered to fight and those who have thronged there to witness the fight look like planets and stars in the blue sky.

The warriors then begin their fight dashing against each. Both being equal, there is no yielding, and they use various trickeries to fell the opponent. The stones they shoot with caterpults go and make dents on palm trees which stand strong and sturdy.

74   *Atumpu*-yellow flowers from the Indian laburnum tree.

75   *Āmpal* – water lily

86-93   The outskirts of *Pukār* and their appended courtyards command the attention of the poet. There lies a slum where pigs with their piglings roam and domestic fowls flutter. The wells are curbed. Bucks and partridges (bird called *Kātai* in Tamil) keep company. Spears are firmed on earth, and shields are positioned in order. These look like the fence built around the memorial stone for those killed in battle. Fishing drails are leaned against narrow-roofed huts. Fishing nets spread for drying on sandy stretches look like the dusky spot on full Moon bright.

94-121   The scene of fisherfolk's merriment and jollity is graphically presented. Fishermen are dark and their hair is red because of not being anointed with oil and is exposed always to salty water. On full moon days they take rest and do not go on the sea for fishing because the sea is rough with high and wide tides, grows black and becomes cold. They avoid brooding over thoughts that would make them emotional. They sport *Ventali* flowers on their person. These flowers are cool and grow abundantly under sheathed pines with hanging roots. To invoke their Sea-God *Varunan*, they install on the ground the horn of pregnant shark. This horn in turn is decked with screw-pine (*talai* in Tamil) flowers. Then they drink palm toddy offered in oblation to the Sea-God. Unto their liking they eat and play and go wherever their craziness directs them.

The sandy shores smell of meat and are strewn with flowers near the firth where the river *Kaviri* merges with the sea of clear water which rises in tides. These tides look like a mountain on whose top black clouds merge and present a scene as if the mountain is blanketed. Further, the scene looks like a child fastening itself to its mother's breasts. The fishfolk then take a dip in the sea to wash their sins off. They bathe further in the river *Kaviri* to rinse their salty skin. Then they play shaking crabs, and dance in the midst of waves; they make dolls of sand and indulge in sensations sweet. In this besotted state, they play with utmost enthusiasm all through the day. *Pukār* is an ancient town sustaining its inveterate tradition. It has flowers in plenty, and can provide unfailingly rare and divine pleasure.

L 97   *Ventali* – a kind of flower known for its cool properties

122-136   In the evenings, when darkness sets in, both men and maidens enjoy good music and watch plays with great enthusiasm. The moonlight exhilarates them. After this, the maidens join their mates in sensual pleasure which makes them drowsy. And in that state they change into homely robes. They avoid taking wine, and instead prefer philtre drinks and sport garlands of their mates who in turn do the same. By this time, it is the last lapse of the night and all go to sleep. Those fishermen who ventured on the sea, look from there to watch the number of lamps which retain brightness by their flames and from this calculate their time for coming back to the shore.

137-148   **Avenue for Revenue** The king's treasures are guarded by men who have taken to an ancient calling of profession collecting toll on goods. These men work without rest and failure and falter not in their job. They are brisk like horses that draw the chariot of the scorching sun. They levy the customs duty in broad streets adjacent to the sea wherein white flowers and sheathed pines lend beauty. They do take rest on the sands which are wavy and fragrant. The waters of the *Kaviri* bring the blooms and lend their fragrance.

149-163   **Description of the Ware House Courtyard** In the expansive and well guarded warehouse, imports from sea are piled up. Unto the sea, articles for export are passed on. Both imports and exports look like clouds that draw water from the sea and rain in torrents which again go to the sea flowing swift. Goods of various sorts arrive at the warehouse. There strong men stamp the Tiger mark and then the goods reach out to the courtyard and are heaped up. Over these heaps, hounds and goats play in jumps. These dogs with clawed nails, and the goat with flexural legs resemble the stags that play on mountain tops and slopes where rainy clouds gather and verdant bamboos long and strong grow rich.

182-210   Hoisting flags for different occasions was a mark of ancient Tamil culture. this continues even unto this day. People invoke blemishless Gods in temples. The entrances are decorated with flowers.

Many flags are hoisted here for the worshippers to offer prayer. The ground is anointed with paste of cowdung, and spears are stood firm on this. Shields are made to rest on these spears. A white flag stands hoisted on these shields which flutters in air. The whiteness of this flag is as bright as sugarcane blooms that gracefully present themselves on the banks of silver sands that the jungle stream brings along with its current.

Items of food are displayed in baskets and rice as white as sugarcane blooms are strewn on them. This signifies that the food is offered to those dead soldiers conceived of as spirits of divine significance. There flaunts yet another flag which signifies that disputes among people are redressed by wise men who infuse respect in those that lack wisdom. *Pukār* being a port town, the ships coming and anchored there have many flags flaunting on their masts. These ships resemble elephants which shake the pegs they are tied to. In the courtyard fish meat is cut, sliced, and fried. Before the toddy shops, on heaps of sand are strewn flowers in offering to Gods. There fly diverse flags of diverse hues and shapes that they scarcely allow the Sun's rays pass through unto earthly objects. These certainly tell of the wealth of *Pukār*.

210   *Pukār* – this is the shortened form of Pūmpukār which is also known as *Kaviri Pūmpaṭṭinam*

211-224   The poet celebrates the wealth of diverse kinds that pile up in *Pukār*. There is an exclusive broad street where goods brought from all directions are stored. As a result, the place always throbs with busy activities. The commodities thus brought make an enchanting blend. Romping horses from aliien lands (Arabia) are imported, sacks and sacks of black pepper arrive from adjacent domestic domain; rare and sparkling gems and dazzling gold find their ways from the Himalayan mounts. *Akil* (eagle-wood) and sandal come from the *Kutaku* region of the western ghats. Pearls and corals from the southward and eastern seas, various other commodities from the beds of the *Ganges* and *Kaviri*, items of food from the Lankan land, and finer things from *Kataram*, gather in the port city. The weight of all these is so huge and the land itself becomes pliable and gets pressed down.

225-240   **Here the Concentration is on the Glory of Peasants**
Peasants in *Pukār* love their job which they do with their plough. Their moral stand is of high order and that is why they extend help to others. They remove murderous intent from murderers and the instinct of thievery from thieves. Since the peasants do perform their job impeccably, the fishfolk and butchers are relieved of their professional imperative. As a result, the fish and cattle stock thrive, abound and play. These peasants pray unto Gods and offer oblation in sacramental fire. They provide security to cows and bullocks. They spread the fame of those versed well in the four *Vetas*. They treat guests with delightful victuals and offer fresh food to almsmen.

238   *Vetas* – the four *Vetas* namely *Rig. Yajur, Sama* and *Atarvana*.

241-247   **Grandeur of Merchants** Merchants in *Pukār* are just in their dealings. They are good hearted with legacy of great wealth. Deviating from the path of justness would result in the destruction of posterity. This thought regulates them and hence they, like the central nail to the lengthy yoke, remain just and tell the truth; they declare open their income and live in assemblies.

248-254   **Description Relating to Harmonious Life of Foreigners in *Pukār*** Just as kinsfolk versed well in various disciplines visiting distant lands and moving in friendship with different people who gather and make merry and change the occasion into one of festivity, there live in *Pukār* people from various countries who blend their mind with joy and love.

255-258   These three lines take a break from the descriptive mode and represent the thematic property-proper of the song. The male lover who is about to depart in search of earnings says unto his lady love that even if he were to be given the town of *Pukār* which throbs with fame and beauty, he would not leave the place thereby leave his lady-love whose hairs are long and dark and who glitters in her bijoutrie.

These lines consolidate the *Akam* in the declaration of the male lover who assures his conscience that even if he were to be endowed with all riches as are found in the heritage town of *Pukār* he would not leave his lady-love for the sake of earning money and set out to alien places. Reverting to the description of external factors that went in the making of *Karikalan* as the King, the poet under the guise of telling reasons for the male lover's glorification of the town *Pukār* (which despite its glory he denies to possess in case of a choice between it and his lady love) devises the description of *Puram*, the external factors. Here starts the dominance of *Aham*, and its supplement *Puram* in the poem.

259-268   Here begins the fame and glory of *Tirumavalavan* (*Karikala Cōlan*), a great King of the early *Cōla* dynasty who in fact is the hero of this long poem. *Uruthiran Kannanar*, the poet hinges on *Tirumavalavan's* prowess and thereby accentuates that this poem celebrates the inner self, its achings, longings, and yearnings. This inner self in Tamil is known as *Akam* which fact precedes the description of King *Karikala Cōlans* heroism.

Description of Karikalan's Ascendence to the Throne
The figurine cub despite being kept in a cage grows without being stunted. Likewise *Karikalan* known as *Tirumavalavan* with the help of his wisdom and valour grew despite captivity by his enemies. He surmounted the secure walls and gained his crown due to him in all respects. In this attempt he resembles the elephant bull which gores the walls of the pit into which it has fallen, and comes out to join its mate.

269-286   **Karikalan's War of Plunder**   *TirumaValavan* did not feel contented with the retrieval of his crown and his right to rule. His craze for war was intense that he surged ahead with elephants characterised by majesty and grace. These elephants with their feet of nails plundered the forts of enemies despite strong security. With their sturdy tusks they broke the massive gates of forts and rolled the diademed heads of enemical kings. Further, with many a horses decorated with precise beads, *Karikalan* sported flowers of varied kinds and looking like a mound went to the war camp where a manmoth drum was kept. Then, after the roar of the drum, he barged into the enemy's camp and made them threadbare to such an extent that eagles began to hover over the corpses of foes. Not satisfied with these exploits, he surged further and went to the arable lands and made the inhabitants migrants. (*Pūlai* – a kind of plant that yields soft cotton).

287-295   The consequence of *Karikālan's* relentless pursuit of enemies resulted in the destruction of arable lands. These lands were rich once with sugar canes with white blooms and paddy. Flowers of varieties such as lilies of different kinds grew so dense and were intertwined. The tanks where alligators once swam with swagger now present a dry look. On the beds of such tanks are to be seen weeds now. There, male deer with ribbed horns do play with their mates.

296-306   Temples were not even spared by the wrath of *Karikālan*. As a result of his frenzied war with enemies, their Queens were taken captives, but were treated respectfully. They did bath in tanks meant only for drinking. Their custom was to lighten the lamps at dusk in the *Sanctum Sanctorum* where the firmed stone stood lending form to formless God. There, people, both aliens and locals flocked to offer worship; such temples did offer lodging to worshippers. In such temples, strong and splendid elephant bulls stand and repose rubbing against pillars and render them weak. All these because such temples were destroyed by the plundering army of *Karikalan*.

307-320   The concert halls were also not spared. The streets which wore a beautiful look with fragrant and rare blooms and pulsated with notes from lyre and consonantal beats on snare drums signifying the on goings of festivals now present a desolate look. In those streets grow now cow's thorn *Nerunchi* and *Aruku* grass. Foxes abound there howling fearsomely which mix with hooting of barn owls. There yelp bitterns. Here both male and female devils roam with horrible looks and dance and eat the corpses of men killed in war.

321-330 **Destruction of Towns of Enemies by the Force of Karikalan find Description in these Lines.**

Mansions with round and shapely pillars accommodated guests without stop and fed them. The large kitchens used to provide food that never went waning. The houses that stood rich with goodly painting and where wealth of milk flowed, and parrots prattled, now stand impoverished where hunters beat their tenor drums and rob the granaries of wealth. Even during daylight barn owls hoot there dirging the disaster wrought.

331-339 **Karikalan's Firm Resolve to Translate His Determination**

The exploits of the king in routing his enemies, and causing havoc are clear evidence of his determination and adroitness which would make him dislodge even mountains, drain the seas, pull down the sky and still the air.

340-352 **Karikalan's Victories**

There is a perfect blend of pride and anger in the king who with the force the blend lends, seizes forts of foes. His valiance, inherent courage, and furious looks at adversaries make them bend in shame, and shiver in fear. The kings of adjacent countries – the ancient *Aruva* land, the northerners, those from the west, the shepherd kings and *Irunkovel* stand helpless, lose their courage, and wait to carry out *Karikālan's* commands. Invariably all these kings are deprived of their lineage.

353-363 In contrast to the destructive deeds of *Karikālan*, these lines celebrate his formative deeds. The King then embarks on destroying forests to establish habitations to failitate people to settle down. He digs ponds and tanks. He extends the city of *Urantai* (now *Woriyur*) and weilds control over temples and citizens and settles them with stability. He devises strong portals and fortfies them with battlements with quivers, all in readiness to attack enemies. His shouts of resolve in fact tone up the spirit of his soldiers who remain determined not to falter in fight. Thus the walls of his fort stand ever blessed with the presence of the Goddess of triumph.

355   *Urantai* – *Woriyur*, the capital of the ancient *Cōla* Kingdom.

364-375 Karikalan's Happy Life is Described

The trammels being over, there prevails happiness in the King which is further augmented by the buckling of some stubborn kings who stand subjugated before him. The beads on the crown of their heads touch the King's feet which look graceful with anklets. The King's sons wearing gold bangles hug him and run here and there. His consort in full glory of her jewellery (bijoutrie) stands close to him that her breasts gently press against his chest smeared with sandal paste. He with jewellery on him stands valiant in which bearing he resembles the lion.

376-379 These lines revert to the *Akam* aspect of this long poem wherein the male lover cites reasons for his remaining at home.

In case he has to go out for earning wealth in alien lands, he will have to pass forests of wilder nature. These forests are far wilder than even the spear of *Tirumavalavan* known as *Karikālan*. But the male lover's lady-love's shoulders are broad and cooler than *Karikālan's* sceptre of right rule. Hence, his preference to stay on.

- --*End*---